MAY 2 2 2012

P9-DHS-489

GUNPOWDER

Chris Oxlade

Heinemann
LIBRARY

Chicago, Illinois

www.heinemannraintree.com
Visit our website to find out
more information about
Heinemann-Raintree books.

To order:
☎ Phone 888-454-2279
🖥 Visit www.heinemannraintree.com
to browse our catalog and order online.

Edited by Louise Galpine and Laura Knowles
Designed by Philippa Jenkins
Original illustrations © Capstone Global Library
    Limited 2012
Picture research by Mica Brancic
Originated by Capstone Global Library Limited
Printed and bound in China by CTPS

15 14 13 12 11
10 9 8 7 6 5 4 3 2 1

Library of Congress Cataloging-in-Publication Data
Cataloging-in-Publication data is available at the Library
of Congress.

ISBN 978 1 4329 5444 4(hardback)
ISBN 978 1 4329 5458 1(paperback)

Acknowledgments
We would like to thank the following for permission
to reproduce photographs: © 2010 The British Library
p. **6**; Alamy pp. **7** (© Interfoto), **9** (© Mary Evans Picture
Library), **27** (© David Hoffman Photo Library); Corbis
pp. **5** (Reuters/© Ivan Alvarado), **13** (© Bettmann), **21**
(© Bettmann), **24** (© PoodlesRock); Getty Images pp.
8 (Science & Society Picture Library), **10** (Roger Viollet
Collection), **14** (The Bridgeman Art Library/Private
Collection/Edward Whymper), **15** (Hulton Archive/FPG/
Jack Zehrt), **17** (Hulton Archive), **18** (Roger Viollet/
Branger), **19** (Hulton Archive), **22** (Archive Photos/
R. Gates), **23** (Time & Life Pictures/Carl Iwasaki);
Photolibrary p. **11** (The British Library); Shutterstock
p. **4** (© Sherri R. Camp).

Cover photograph of women from Brook's fireworks
factory, one of the oldest British fireworks companies,
showing off a selection of their huge rockets and
Catherine wheels (early 1930s), reproduced with
permission of Mary Evans Picture Library.

We would like to thank Peter Smithurst for his
invaluable help in the preparation of this book.

Every effort has been made to contact copyright holders
of material reproduced in this book. Any omissions will
be rectified in subsequent printings if notice is given to
the publisher.

CONTENTS

Look for these boxes

Biographies

These boxes tell you about the life of inventors, the dates when they lived, and their important discoveries.

Setbacks

Here we tell you about the experiments that didn't work, the failures, and the accidents.

EUREKA!

These boxes tell you about important events and discoveries, and what inspired them.

Any words appearing in the text in bold, **like this**, are explained in the glossary.

TIMELINE

2011—The timeline shows you when important discoveries and inventions were made.

WHAT IS GUNPOWDER?

The bangs and flashes of fireworks are made by a special mixture—gunpowder. In a large fireworks display, many tons of gunpowder will explode. These displays are normally the only places we see gunpowder at work. But gunpowder is also used in mines to break up rocks and in guns to fire bullets. In fact, that is how it got its name.

Spectacular fireworks displays rely on gunpowder.

What is gunpowder made of?

Gunpowder is an **explosive**. It is made up of three ingredients—**charcoal**, **sulfur**, and a chemical called potassium nitrate, or **saltpeter**. When gunpowder is heated up, these ingredients react together and . . . bang! The mixture explodes, giving off gas, smoke, and light.

around 100 CE—Chinese **alchemists** experiment with saltpeter (see page 6)

Explosives

Gunpowder is known as a **low explosive**. It burns quickly, but not suddenly. **Explosives** that burn suddenly are called **high explosives**. They are used in mining, building, and demolition work. Dynamite and TNT are examples of high explosives.

Setbacks

Even though gunpowder is a low explosive, it is still extremely dangerous. That is why there are warnings on fireworks packages. On May 13, 2000, a fire started in a fireworks factory in Enschede, in the Netherlands. The fire **ignited** 195 tons of fireworks, creating a blast that flattened houses all around the factory.

Here, rock is being blasted to pieces with high explosives at a copper mine.

around 600–900 CE—
Black powder is used to make fireworks in China (see page 6)

BLACK POWDER

The first kind of gunpowder was called black powder. We don't know when it was first invented. However, we do know Chinese **alchemists** knew about **saltpeter** in the 100s CE, during the Han dynasty.

Gunpowder was probably used in fireworks during the Tang dynasty (618–907 CE). It was certainly being used in China to make simple guns and bombs by the 900s CE. The guns were called fire lances. They were made of a bamboo stick with gunpowder pushed into it, which fired a metal ball. The Chinese also fired bombs called *fei-huo* or "flying fires" by catapult, and they made rockets and **land mines** (underground bombs).

This spinning wheel **explosive** was one of the weapons used in China in the 900s.

Setbacks

Accidents with gunpowder started almost as soon as it was discovered. A Chinese **manuscript** (early book) written in the 9th century says that some alchemists "have been burned, and even the whole house where they worked burned down".

Keeping a secret

The Chinese wanted to keep gunpowder a secret! In the 1000s CE, leaders of the Song dynasty tried to stop traders from selling saltpeter and **sulfur** to foreigners (people from another country). But the secret leaked out. Over the next 200 years, word of gunpowder spread along trade routes, such as the **Silk Road** in China, into India, the Arab World, and eventually to Europe.

A German monk named Berthold Schwarz experimented with gunpowder in the 1350s.

EUREKA!

Gunpowder was almost certainly invented by luck. Two ingredients of gunpowder—saltpeter and sulfur—were ingredients in ancient Chinese medicine. It is likely that somebody accidentally set off an explosion while preparing medicines.

around 900 CE—Black powder is used in simple guns and bombs in China

1044—A Chinese manuscript describes recipes for gunpowder (see page 8)

1100s—Knowledge of gunpowder spreads to India, the Arab world, and Europe

Making black powder

Black powder was made from saltpeter, **charcoal**, and sulfur. These were ground up and mixed together. Some of the earliest gunpowder recipes come from a Chinese manuscript called the *Wujing Zongyao*, written in 1044. The manuscript has recipes to make gunpowder for explosive bombs and for poisonous **smoke bombs**.

This drawing shows a man testing saltpeter, one of the ingredients of gunpowder, in the 1500s.

around 1240s—
Gunpowder is used for the first time in Europe

1242—
Roger Bacon describes gunpowder

around 1267—
Corned powder, a sort of gunpowder paste, is developed

Roger Bacon *an English man*

EUREKA!

One day, somebody discovered that using urine instead of water made corned gunpowder explode better. Apparently the urine from people who drank beer was best!

In 1242 English scientist Roger Bacon wrote down a recipe for gunpowder.

Corned powder

In Europe, gunpowder is thought to have first been used around the 1240s. Early gunpowder was a dry mixture. It had to be remixed before using it because the ingredients slowly separated. By 1267 the ingredients were mixed with water to make a thick paste. The paste was dried and broken into granules. This gunpowder was known as corned powder.

Setbacks

Corned powder exploded with much more force than dry powder. If it was used in old **cannons**, the explosion sometimes blew the cannons to pieces!

9

1605—The Gunpowder Plot to blow up the English Houses of **Parliament** is uncovered before harm is done (see page 11)

1681—The Canal du Midi, France, is completed using gunpowder to blast through rock (see page 14)

THE GUNPOWDER REVOLUTION

The invention of gunpowder allowed the invention of weapons, such as **cannons** and **muskets**. These weapons completely changed how soldiers fought battles. Before this, soldiers had to throw weapons such as spears, or they fired arrows from bows. With weapons that used gunpowder, soldiers could attack from farther away.

Thick castle walls were no defense against cannonballs launched by gunpowder. The balls smashed holes in walls that attackers could march through. Musket balls traveled so fast it was impossible to see them coming, and they did terrible damage. Traditional knights, who were used to hand-to-hand fighting with swords, thought that muskets made the fight unfair!

Here, a French soldier can be seen ramming gunpowder into a cannon.

1775—Britain cuts off gunpowder supplies to the American **colonies**. Antoine Lavoisier takes charge of gunpowder production in France. The Revolutionary War begins (see page 12).

Robert Winter

Christopher Wright

Iohn Wright

Thomas Percy

Guido Fawkes

Robert Catesby

Thomas Winter

In 1605 Robert Catesby, Guy Fawkes, and others tried to blow up England's King James I in the English **Parliament**. They secretly piled 36 barrels of gunpowder in a cellar under the Parliament buildings. But the gunpowder was discovered, and the gang was arrested. The "Gunpowder Plot" is remembered in the United Kingdom with bonfires and fireworks on November 5 each year.

These men were the ringleaders of the Gunpowder Plot of 1605. Guy Fawkes was also known as Guido.

Gunpowder supplies

Cutting off the enemy's gunpowder supplies soon became a tactic (plan) of war. Just before the Revolutionary War (1775–83), the British stopped supplying gunpowder to the American **colonies**. The colonies had to find somewhere else to get gunpowder so that they would be able to fight against their British enemies.

France to the rescue

The Americans couldn't make enough gunpowder themselves in their own gunpowder mills. Luckily the French came to their rescue. In 1775 the famous French chemist Antoine Lavoisier was put in charge of gunpowder production in France. Soon France was making enough gunpowder not only for its own army, but also for the Americans.

Setbacks

Gunpowder was extremely powerful. However, there were problems with using it in weapons. Gunpowder made lots of smoke when it exploded. During battles, the air quickly filled with smoke. Because of this, **musketeers** struggled to see their targets, and the smoke from their muskets gave away their hiding places.

Thick gunpowder smoke drifted across the battlefield at Gettysburg, Pennsylvania, during the Civil War.

The Battle of the Crater

The supply of gunpowder also played a part in the American Civil War (1861–65). The destructive power of gunpowder was demonstrated at the Battle of the Crater in 1864. The **Union** army tunneled under the **Confederate** defenses at Petersburg, Virginia. Union soldiers put 3,600 kilograms (7,900 pounds) of gunpowder in place. The explosion killed hundreds of Confederate soldiers and left a crater 51 meters (167 feet) long, 18 meters (59 feet) wide, and 9 meters (30 feet) deep. It can still be seen today.

1825—The Erie Canal is completed in the United States (see page 14)

Mining and tunneling

Until the 1800s, miners broke up rocks by bashing them hard or by heating and then cooling them, again and again. Then somebody thought of blasting rocks apart with gunpowder. **Coal** miners used gunpowder to blast the rocks apart, so they could easily scoop up the shattered coal.

Railroads and canals

Gunpowder was also important in building work on railroads and canals. One of the earliest projects to make use of gunpowder was the Canal du Midi in France, completed in 1681. Later, engineers used gunpowder to blast a way for the Erie Canal in New York, which opened in 1825.

These workers are drilling holes for **explosives** in the Mont Cenis Tunnel, France, around 1868.

1831—William Bickford invents the safety fuse

Risky business

Blasting with gunpowder was a risky business. First, miners or tunnelers drilled holes and filled them with gunpowder (called the **charge**). Then they laid a fuse. This was a thin trail of gunpowder leading away from the charge. When the fuse was lit, the flame ran along the trail to the charge. But sometimes the trail burned too quickly, and men were killed or injured when the gunpowder exploded before they could run away.

Here, workers are placing explosives deep underground in an iron mine in the 1880s.

EUREKA!

Miners tried various sorts of fuses, but accidents kept happening. William Bickford was worried about the number of miners killed in tin mines in England. In 1831 he invented a safety fuse. It was made up of twisted string containing gunpowder and coated in tar. This new fuse stopped the gunpowder from being **ignited** by accident.

1845—Christian Schönbein discovers **nitrocellulose** by accident (see page 16)

1846—Ascanio Sobrero invents nitroglycerine (see page 20)

REPLACING BLACK POWDER

Black powder was the only **explosive** that existed until the middle of the 1800s. Then, in 1845, German chemist Christian Schönbein made an important discovery. He found that cotton fibers dipped in a chemical called nitric acid became explosive. We now call this explosive material **nitrocellulose**. At first the material was unstable—it burst into flames without warning.

EUREKA!

Schönbein often performed his chemistry experiments at home in his kitchen (even though his wife told him not to). One day, he spilled a bottle of nitric acid onto the kitchen table. He wiped it up with a cotton apron and hung the apron by the stove. As soon as the apron was dry and warm, it burst into flames. The cotton in the apron had turned into the explosive nitrocellulose.

Nitrocellulose

Schönbein invented a way of making nitrocellulose a bit safer. He dipped cotton in a mixture of **sulfuric acid** and nitric acid for two minutes. Then, he rinsed the cotton with cold water and dried it carefully.

Guncotton

Nitrocellulose was tried as gunpowder from the 1860s. It was given the name guncotton. It could fire bullets faster from rifles. However, it was dangerous to make and handle and caused many accidents, including explosions in factories where it was made.

1860s— Nitrocellulose is used to make gunpowder

1862—Alfred Nobel begins experimenting with nitroglycerine (see page 20)

Christian Schönbein (1799–1868)

Christian Schönbein was a German chemist who taught in England and Switzerland. In addition to discovering nitrocellulose, Schönbein also did research on iron and hydrogen peroxide (bleach) and published many scientific papers during his life. Around 1840, he also discovered and named the gas ozone. He named it after the Greek word *ozein*, which means "to smell," because the gas had a strange smell.

1864—In Virginia, **Union** soldiers explode a huge gunpowder **land mine** under **Confederate** lines at the Battle of the Crater (see page 13)

1865— Alfred Nobel invents the blasting cap (see page 24)

1866— Nobel invents dynamite (see page 23)

1867— Nobel is granted a **patent** for dynamite

1875— Nobel invents gelignite (see page 24)

A safer explosive

In the 1880s, French chemist Paul Vieille invented a new **manufacturing** process. This process made nitrocellulose much safer to make and use. He added chemicals called stabilizers, which stopped it from exploding suddenly if it got warm. Vieille's new gunpowder was known as *Poudre B*.

These are the twisted remains of the French Battleship *Liberté*, accidently blown up by *Poudre B*.

Setbacks

Even after Paul Vieille's work, gunpowders based on nitrocellulose were not perfectly safe. The French navy lost two battleships—the *Iéna* (in 1907) and the *Liberté* (in 1911)—and hundreds of sailors when unstable *Poudre B* blew up unexpectedly.

1880s—Paul Vieille invents a new nitrocellulose gunpowder known as *Poudre B*

1886—The French army begins using *Poudre B*

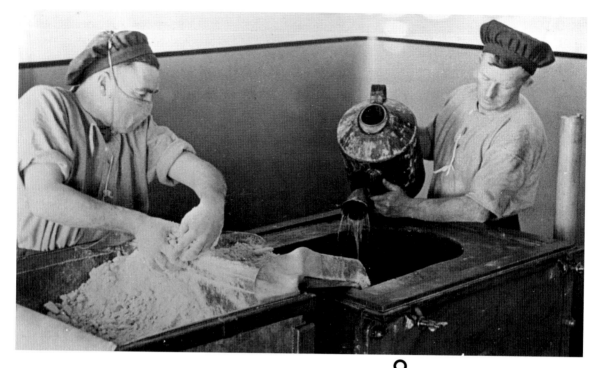

These workers are manufacturing cordite, an explosive similar to *Poudre B*.

Other gunpowders

The French army began using *Poudre B* in 1886. Around this time, other similar gunpowders were also developed. *Ballistite* was invented by Alfred Nobel, and cordite was invented by Frederick Abel for the British army.

Smokeless powder

The nitrocellulose explosive made by Vieille was far better than black powder. When the nitrocellulose explosive burned it just produced gases, which pushed bullets and shells from their guns very fast. There was also no smoke, which is why it became known as smokeless powder.

Setbacks

Nitrocellulose was an ingredient in one of the first plastics, called celluloid. For many decades movie film was made from celluloid. However, this could be dangerous, as film regularly burst into flames.

NITROGLYCERINE

Nitroglycerine is one of the most powerful **high explosives**. Its power comes from the huge volume of gas it produces instantly when it explodes. It was invented in 1846 by Italian chemist Ascanio Sobrero. He mixed a chemical called glycerol with nitric acid and **sulfuric acid**. Sobrero called it pyroglycerin. It was also known as "blasting oil" because of its oily feel.

However, nitroglycerine had a major drawback. It was very sensitive to shock. If a drop of nitroglycerine fell to the ground, it exploded instantly. This meant nitroglycerine was too dangerous to use instead of gunpowder.

Alfred Nobel and nitroglycerine

In 1862 the Swedish chemist Alfred Nobel and his father, Immanuel, began experimenting with nitroglycerine. Nobel had learned about the power of nitroglycerine when he met Sobrero in Paris. He realized it would be a perfect **explosive** for blasting tunnels and making railroad paths through hills and mountains. Nobel set to work to find a way to stop nitroglycerine from exploding suddenly.

Setbacks

Nobel's experiments with nitroglycerine caused several explosions. In 1864 his nitroglycerine factory in Stockholm, Sweden, blew up. The explosion killed several people, including Alfred's brother, Emil.

1907—The French battleship *Iéna* is destroyed by an explosion of *Poudre B* (see page 18)

1911—The French Battleship *Liberté* is destroyed by an explosion of *Poudre B* (see page 18)

The Hoosac Tunnel opened in 1875 in Massachusetts. It was the first tunnel blasted with nitroglycerine.

Keep trying

Alfred Nobel knew that nitroglycerine was very dangerous. If the explosive liquid was handled carelessly, it could easily explode. But Nobel formed a company to make it anyway. Several more accidents followed, including one that destroyed Nobel's factory in Krümmel, Germany, in 1866.

Nobel kept experimenting, trying to find a way to make nitroglycerine safer. He was banned from continuing his dangerous work in Stockholm, so he carried out his experiments on a boat on the Elbe River. This meant that any explosions would not harm other people.

Dynamite

In 1866 Nobel discovered that mixing nitroglycerine with a type of earth, known as *kieselguhr* (or just "guhr"), made a paste. The paste was not as likely to burst into flames as plain nitroglycerine, and it did not explode if it was dropped. In 1867 Alfred Nobel **patented** this new explosive. He named it dynamite. Nobel's first sort of dynamite, called *dynamite no.1*, was 75 percent nitroglycerine and 25 percent guhr. It was shaped into rods known as sticks of dynamite.

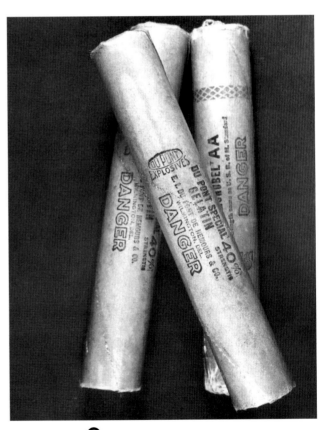

Dynamite was made into sticks like these.

EUREKA!

Around the time that Nobel was inventing dynamite, pneumatic (air-powered) drills were developed for drilling into rock. This was a handy coincidence. To blast rock, holes could be drilled quickly with a pneumatic drill and filled with sticks of dynamite. This made blasting in mines and tunnels much faster and cheaper and, just as importantly, much safer.

Dynamite is used for demolition. Here, a giant factory chimney is shattered by the power of dynamite.

NOBEL'S EXPLOSIVES

Alfred Nobel's inventions made **explosives** far more powerful than before, but also safer. Dynamite quickly replaced gunpowder as the explosive for miners and engineers. It was the first safe, powerful explosive, and it saved many lives.

In 1865 Nobel created a **detonator** called a blasting cap, designed to blast off dynamite. It was a small metal cap that exploded when it was heated or hit very hard.

In 1875 Nobel mixed nitroglycerine with the chemical collodion and made an explosive that was like putty. It was even more powerful than dynamite. He called the new material gelignite.

This diagram shows a simple blasting cap of the type invented by Nobel.

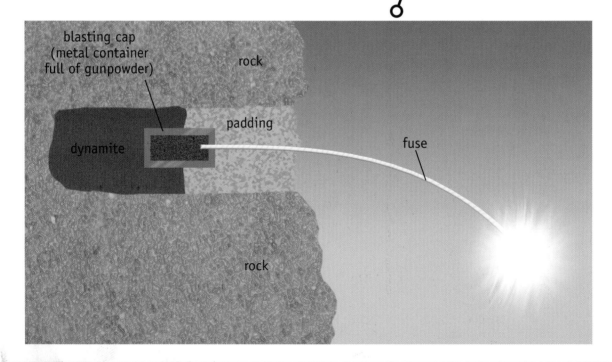

blasting cap
(metal container
full of gunpowder)

rock

padding

dynamite

fuse

rock

1958—A massive **charge** of **high explosive** blasts away an underwater rock in Canada (see page 26)

Alfred Nobel (1833–1896)

Alfred Nobel was born in Stockholm, Sweden. His father, Immanuel, had used gunpowder for blasting rocks and making sea mines (underwater bombs). While in Paris, France, Nobel met the man who discovered nitroglycerine, Ascanio Sobrero (see page 20). In the 1850s and 1860s, he worked with his father on developing nitroglycerine as a usable explosive.

Nobel's big breakthrough was inventing dynamite. He was a good businessman and made a fortune from his invention. When Nobel died, he left money to be awarded to outstanding people in the worlds of science, medicine, literature, and peace. These prizes are now known as the Nobel prizes.

GUNPOWDER TODAY

There have been dozens of **explosives** inventions within the last 150 years. So you might be surprised to learn that black powder is still used today. It is mostly used in fireworks, but it is also used in **detonators**, fuses, emergency **flares**, and **blank rounds** in guns.

Modern explosives

In blasting, gunpowder has been replaced by **high explosives**, including dynamite, SEMTEX®, and TNT (short for trinitrotoluene). However, the **manufacture** of explosives uses large amounts of chemicals. There is always a chance of chemicals leaking into the air. There is the added danger of accidental explosions, such as the one at Enschede in the Netherlands (see page 5).

Fun fireworks

All explosives produce a large amount of noise. This becomes a problem for people if explosions are very loud or repeated often. We call this "noise pollution." Some people complain about the noise of fireworks displays. However, for most people throughout the history of gunpowder, fireworks have been the fun side of explosives.

EUREKA!

The power of explosives was demonstrated with the biggest bang of all time (not including wars), which was set off in 1958. A massive 1,381 tons of Nitramex high explosive blew the top off an underwater rock in Canada. This was to allow ships to pass safely over the rock.

High explosives are now used to demolish large buildings, such as these apartment buildings.

2000—An explosion destroys
a fireworks factory in
Enschede, Netherlands
(see page 5)

TIMELINE

around 100 CE
Chinese **alchemists** experiment with **saltpeter**

around 600–900 CE
Black powder is used to make fireworks in China

around 900 CE
Black powder is used in simple guns and bombs in China

1775
Antoine Lavoisier takes charge of gunpowder production in France

1775
Britain cuts off gunpowder supplies to the American **colonies**

1681
The Canal du Midi, France, is completed using gunpowder to blast through rock

1775
The Revolutionary War begins

1825
The Erie Canal is completed in New York

1831
William Bickford invents the safety fuse

1875
Nobel invents gelignite

1867
Nobel is granted a **patent** for dynamite

1866
Nobel invents dynamite

1880s
Paul Vieille invents a new nitrocellulose gunpowder known as *Poudre B*

1886
The French army begins using *Poudre B*

1907
The French battleship *Iéna* is destroyed by an explosion of *Poudre B*

1044
A Chinese **manuscript** describes recipes for gunpowder

1100s
Knowledge of gunpowder spreads to India, the Arab world, and Europe

around 1240s
Gunpowder is used for the first time in Europe

1605
The Gunpowder Plot (to blow up the English Houses of **Parliament**) is uncovered before harm is done

1267
Corned powder, a sort of gunpowder paste, is developed

1242
Roger Bacon describes gunpowder

1845
Christian Schöbein discovers **nitrocellulose** by accident

1846
Ascanio Sobrero invents nitroglycerine

1860s
Nitrocellulose is used to make gunpowder

1865
Alfred Nobel invents the blasting cap

1864
In Virginia, **Union** soldiers explode a huge gunpowder **land mine** under **Confederate** lines at the Battle of the Crater

1862
Alfred Nobel begins experimenting with nitroglycerine

1911
The French battleship *Liberté* is destroyed by an explosion of *Poudre B*

1958
A massive **charge** of **high explosive** blasts away an underwater rock in Canada

2000
An explosion destroys a fireworks factory in Enschede, Netherlands

GLOSSARY

alchemist person from medieval times who tried to make new materials (such as gold) from other natural materials

blank round cartridge (for a gun) that does not have a bullet in it

cannon old type of large gun that fired heavy metal balls (cannonballs)

charcoal black, brittle material made by burning wood in only a little air

charge quantity of explosive that will be blown up

coal hard, black material that is mined from rocks and burned as fuel

colony area of land controlled by a country, normally a long way away from that country

Confederate short for the Confederate States of America, which was formed by 11 southern U.S. states in the 1860s, and fought against the Union side in the American Civil War

detonator small explosive charge that sets off a larger amount of explosive

explosive any material that is designed to explode

flare special sort of firework used to signal for help in an emergency

high explosive material that explodes instantly, creating a powerful shockwave

ignite light up or set on fire

land mine bomb that is buried secretly underground, designed to blow up anything that goes over it

low explosive material that explodes because it burns very quickly, but not instantly

manufacture make something in large numbers

manuscript document, normally written on paper

musket old type of gun that fired small, round metal balls (musket balls)

musketeer soldier who fought using a musket

nitrocellulose sort of gunpowder made from cotton fibers

parliament group of people who make some countries' laws

patent official proof that an invention, idea, or process was the idea of a particular person. It protects it from being copied.

saltpeter material found on cave walls and in decaying animal droppings. It can also be made from other chemicals.

Silk Road ancient trading route between the Mediterranean and China, named because silk was moved along it from China to Europe

smoke bomb explosive device designed to make lots of smoke rather than blow something up

sulfur soft, yellow mineral found in the ground

sulfuric acid liquid that dissolves some materials and can burn skin

Union collection of northern U.S. states that fought against the Confederate side in the American Civil War

FIND OUT MORE

Books

Oxlade, Chris. *Inventors' Secret Scrapbook* (*Crabtree Connections*). New York: Crabtree, 2011.

Rau, Dana Meachen. *Fireworks* (*Surprising Science*). New York: Marshall Cavendish Benchmark, 2011.

Trueit, Trudi Strain. *Gunpowder* (*Inventions That Shaped the World*). New York: Franklin Watts, 2005.

Websites

www.hagley.org/library/exhibits/civilwartech
The Hagley Museum and Library website has information on gunpowder use in the American Civil War.

http://nobelprize.org/alfred_nobel
Visit the official Nobel Prize website to find biographical information about Alfred Nobel.

Places to visit

The National Civil War Museum
One Lincoln Circle at Reservoir Park
Harrisburg, Pennsylvania 17103
www.nationalcivilwarmuseum.org
This museum explores the American Civil War and features displays of weapons used during the war.

Petersburg National Battlefield
5001 Siege Road
Petersburg, Virginia 23803
www.nps.gov/pete/index.htm
Visit the location of the Battle of the Crater and learn more about the American Civil War in this historic area.

INDEX